TOP SECRETS of JOINT VENTURES

TOP SECRETS of JOINT VENTURES

Contents

Disclaimer 1
Contents 3
What Is A Joint Venture? 5
Reasons To Join In A Joint Venture 7
How To Find A Joint Venture Partner To Promote Your Product 11
How Does a Joint Venture Boost Online Sales? 14
How to Find and Cut A Joint Venture Deal Just Like A Professional 17
How Do You Know You Are Ready For An Online Joint Venture? 20
Looking At The Joint Venture As A Process 23
Who To Go After As A Joint Venture Partner 26
Joint Ventures And Face To Face Encounters 29
Three Key Elements to Making Your Online Joint Venture Successful 32
Setting Up Competitive Barriers with Your Joint Venture Partner 35
Tools For Picking Out The Right Joint Venture Partner For You 38
Creativity, Persistence, And Vision 41
Joint Venture Partnerships Without You Having A Product 44
Using Free Products To Use As A Joint Venture 46
More Benefits of Joint Marketing Ventures 49
When To Enter A Joint Venture With Caution 53
How To Avoid Legal Issues In Your Joint Venture 56
Personal Success Stories With Joint Venture Partners 60
    That's One Spicy Sauce! 60
    Fashion Is A Must 61
    You Sell Butterflies? 62
    Music Enthusiast Make Big 63

Home With the Kids and Still Working 64
What Have We Learned About Joint Venture Partnerships 67
Useful Resources You *Really* Should Check Out!... 69

What Is A Joint Venture?

A joint venture, defined by Webster's is an entity formed between two or more parties to undertake an economic activity together. The parties that wish to form this group, though separate at the beginning of the venture, makes agreed upon allowances in work division and economic contributions.

The venture is usually for one specific project only and usually the venture will break once that particular job is done. Sometimes the ventures, if successful, will come together as a continued venture in another line of direction or the venture will follow the same line, but will end when the venture goal ends.

There is equity in states when a joint venture becomes solidified. If there were no equity in states then the joint venture would be called a strategic alliance and the alliance is not as rigid both economically and physically as a joint venture. A joint venture may be a corporation in which duel agreed upon investments in money and time are agreed on or there is a lesser form where one partner will have a limited liability than t he other. The joint venture can be called a partnership, but the legal structure of a partnership would hold each party liable equally in case of civil or criminal litigation. Joint ventures are common in the gas and oil industry, but they are often done on a much smaller scale. Sometimes two business men will just agree to come together to market a certain product or to do research and development that will benefit both. Joint ventures have a fairly low rate of success if geographic location, communication, and all avenues of business is not planned and implemented from the start. Joint ventures do well in third world countries where the substance of one man cannot compete with the local economy without the assistance of another. In industrial countries, the idea of a joint venture is to use the other partner's materials, money, expertise, or marketing outlets to further the ambitions of the first partner.

The negative aspect of a joint venture is that if the product is technologically based, then most partnerships cannot keep up with the technological changes in the makeup of the product or the structure of the joint venture prohibits the product to keep up with competition due to marketing strategies and initial marketing output. Because of this many countries such as China and India require that joint ventures have to be formed with domestic companies in their home country before they can enter the market for that particular product. This is due to the high failure rate of joint ventures with outside companies due to cultural differences, language, currency, and other factors that limit productivity and marketing.

Joint ventures on a small scale with two experienced partners have shown to be very compatible with today's markets and have proven that they can stand the test of time if the agreement is comprehensive and both partners uphold their end of the bargain. The joint venture can bring a company to the next level of competition or get a product out faster and more efficiently than if the single partner tried to do it on their own. It is advisable to include your lawyer in the negotiations at the planning phase of the joint venture. Without the legal advice it could be more expensive down the road to quell in legal problems.

Reasons To Join In A Joint Venture

There are many reasons to come into a joint venture and most are categorized into three categories. The first is internal reasons. The internal makeup of a company may not be able to get the company goal completed without the help of another company. By sharing the vision and the profit, the company can use another company's assets and materials to bring the vision to be without adding expenditure and restructuring of the original company.

One of the internal reasons to join in a joint venture is to build on the companies strengths. If you are marketing an e-book or other internet related properties, you might have a good customer base. To go into a joint venture with a partner who has experience selling and marketing on the internet, your company's strengths will be higher, because you can use the reputation and the know how of your joint venture partner to boost the integrity of your company. Your profit is a direct reflection to the strength of your company and to use the other guy's knowledge and strength to build your own just makes good business sense.

Another internal reason to go into a joint venture is to spread out the costs and the risks of your goal. If you are short of capital and you need the extra money to start your marketing strategy, than the money or capital of the joint venture partner will strengthen your plan. By having the joint venture partner absorb the costs of the initial marketing campaign, you will use less of your capital and, in return, you take less of a risk in losing that capital. If your product does not sell or if there is some faux pas in the plan, you lose what you invested and the partner will lose his share and you will both still be in business.

When taking on a new project and securing financial resources, it is wise to use someone else's credit if your credit is not adequate in covering the costs. If your proposed joint venture partner has better credit or other financial resources, you can adjust apart of your profit to give them in exchange for their good financial credit and backing. You could apply and get new loans, go to different companies with financial backing, and you could look better on your portfolio.

Your joint venture partner may have the financial backing to finance the entire project, but expect a large portion of the profits to go to the person putting in the most money.

I'm bigger therefore I win. This sentiment can be explained by having both companies and partners merging to become a bigger impact maker in the market. The bigger you are, the more you will be noticed and seen by potential customers as someone with a solid foothold in the business. They won't see you as a fly by night person that will promise goods and services and then not deliver. Over thirty percent of marketing failures come from the business not being in business long enough or the power of the name backing the business not having enough clout to complete in the market.

A fourth internal reason to go into a joint venture is the size advantage. If you and your partner pool your customers, your customer base will be larger and the potential for higher profits will be greater. Another advantage of size would be that there would be more potential for public awareness. A business that is joint ventured with another one enjoys more prestige because of the increased customer base and the increased selling power and services in now offers. Size gains attention because most clients and services would rather do business with a larger, established giant, then the Jack that most small businesses are considered.

That last two reasons for an internal joint venture is to innovate the managerial practices and to bring in new technologies. Even on a small scale, say if you are an author, you may have the product, the written text, but you may not have the technology or the know how to get the book printed, published, and marketed. A joint venture with an individual or a company that has expertise in these things will give you the means and the competitive edge to be able to get that book to market and to start you on your way to making a profit.

The next category for reasons for a joint venture is for competitive reasons or goals. If you have a prototype product that will revolutionize an aspect of the industry, you need the size and the clout to get this new product to market. With a joint venture partner, you can combine resources and knowledge to lead this cutting edge technology to the markets you want to cover and at the same time you want to be able to have enough persuasion to break into existing companies in which your product would benefit.

A joint venture can also pre-empt your competition. If you have a competitor at the same financial strength that you have and one that has the same resources and skills, the joint venture partner that you bring into the deal may have more skill and resources and you can beat your competition to the punch and rake in the benefits of having your product or service on the market before them. The product will also be seen as an innovation when it comes out with the right marketing and the right time.

A joint venture can also make your partnership a stronger competitive unit than either business that stands alone. The integrity and strength of your company lies on your bottom line of profit versus deficit. With a stronger base of the combined companies, you will be able to over run and over step the advances of your competitor and in an open marketing battle, you will be able to persuade a lending institution or a larger marketing firm to go on your side of the argument versus the side of your competitor.

You will be able to get your products to market faster if you pick a joint venture partner that has marketing capabilities. If you are lacking in anything that would hinder your product's progress, you need to find that weakness and supplement with the strength of your future joint venture partner. This will improve your agility in the market and at the same time, you will be able to use your new found ally to find new markets and to flood the ones that you have already structured.

The last category is self-explanatory. Diversification leads to productivity and higher success. If you have a joint venture partner that has the tools you need, you product and your goal can diversify to meet the needs of your clients.

How To Find A Joint Venture Partner To Promote Your Product

Now that you know what a joint venture is and how it can help you promote your business or product, the question now is, "Where do I find a joint venture partner?" There are several places to find a partner and this chapter will give you the best resources in finding the right joint venture partner for you that is best for your ideas of business and your business needs. No matter what venue you choose, have a plan before you go into a conversation with a potential partner.

The best venue is offline resources. Seminars, conferences, and tradeshows offer many opportunities of other people that are of a like mind. Get to know the people at these events. They may not be able to help you now, but they can be a resource in the future. Trade business cards and keep them on your rolodex. You can always go back and find that promising person if the need arises. Go to as many public get-togethers as you can and make yourself and your business known. There may even be people that might want to use your company and your skill to become a joint venture partner for their product or service.

You might want to use services like Click Bank or other kinds of network affiliates that are willing to promote your product. Other services like Google ads and yahoo have mass media contacts that can get your product to more internet sites and give you more exposure. Though not an official joint venture partner, you can network and find someone that is familiar with these venues. Make sure they have been in business for awhile and have a successful track record. Look at a future joint venture partner like most other companies look at you.

Search engines are a choice but you need to search for your competition as well as a joint venture partner. Make sure that your potential partner does not have affiliations with a competitor. This could lead to a business conflict and a potential legal problem down the road. Find your niche and go with it. Don't just depend on the first couple of pages of hits you get. Most of these are there because of keyword stuffing or written articles that are strategically placed to get your attention and business. Dive deeper and check out sites that are found on page five and six of your keyword search.

There are networks for joint ventures on the web that allows you to post your idea for a joint venture and let interested parties contact you. This is a good system but beware. Sometimes you will be contacted by people that do not have your best interest in mind. Investigate their backgrounds and find out if they are truly authentic. When you are putting your idea on the web, you are also putting your idea open to your competitors. They could easily still your marketing ideas and put them up for their own stealing your profit and your jump on the market.

Myface.com and Myspace.com are good social networks to find a partner if you are in the right circles. Again be careful who you pitch your ideas to. The person might be trying to network to find out how to market their product and your proposal could give them all the information they need.

How Does a Joint Venture Boost Online Sales?

By using a joint venture you can enhance the relationship of your subscribers or future customers on your website. If you have a product or service that is unique or if your product has a price that will draw customers, then joint venturing is the best way to increase your online sales.

You have to convince the customer that you are going out of the way to give them a deal or offer them something that they can't go without. They have to see the worth of your product or they may think that you are trying to cheat them.

When you increase the size of your investment or opt-in, you are automatically increasing the size of your subscribers. If you are joint venturing with one specific site or a network of sites, you potential to add hundreds and perhaps thousands of potential subscribers can happen within minutes or hours. As the subscriber base increases, you might want to promote the person that you are in a joint venture with. You can watch each others back and trade off good clientele with a good word passed on about your partner. This kind of relationship reciprocates and your good name will be passed on also.

As your partner passes on your good name, your creditability will grow as well as your customer base. Gaining credibility and goodwill between the partnerships creates trust within the joint venture and gives the customer a feeling of trust and well being seeing the partners back up each other. If there is a one sided good will credit being given and it is not reciprocated, then the customer will be put off and both companies and parties will suffer. It's like going into a restaurant and seeing the employees having a good time and being proud of their service and product. Seeing this, you want to be a customer again and again.

Your customers trust you now and stay with you because you have done the right in the past and they are happy with your product or service. When you pass on the good name of your partner, that trust goes with it. You have to have a partner that will live up to that trust because if your partner does your subscriber wrong, you will lose that customer. The same reciprocation goes on with you. Your partner is giving you're the benefit of the doubt, and if you screw up, then you both lose a customer. It is a lose-lose situation if one of the other of you lets down the customer. You both are left empty handed and it may cause both of your interests to suffer.

A recidivating joint venture is a great way to boost your online sales without really putting anything out there in the financial realm. It allows you to get in and take your partners traffic and at the same time you don't have to spend money to get new traffic in. This way you will not take the risk of having to lose all your money if no traffic is generated.

The last reason a joint venture boosts online sales is that you can offer your partners products on your site and they can offer yours or theirs. This way you have two sites carrying your name and your products, doubling your exposure and letting you increase sales with no or very little loss of money.

How to Find and Cut A Joint Venture Deal Just Like A Professional

The first thing you need to consider when planning on a joint venture is to find a partner out there that sells similar items that you are selling. For example, if you sell used books online and you have an inventory on your site of a thousand books, you need to find someone as large as you are or larger and post your books on their site and their books on yours. This way the used book buying public will have double the chance of exposure of both your sites and all of your books. This will drive up sales for both partners without investing anything into the venture.

If you are a reputable company and sale high quality products, you need to find the same kind of company with similar products. You should look for someone that has been in business for some time and has a customer base that can be exploited. At the same time you have to offer yourself up as the same kind of trustworthy company and be ready for your joint venture partner to exploit from you. Exploit is a harsh word, but the idea is the same. You are both using each other in a symbiotic relationship not for survival, but for the continuation of a successful business.

For example, if you sell pet name tags on your site and you call up a site that sells dog collars, you can go into a joint venture with them offering their collars on your site and your tags on their's. You both have a win-win situation because you both have a customer base of pet owners.

Your products compliment each other and if your tags are sold, so might be a collar to put it on. Vice versa, if your partner sells a collar, you might get a sale on the tag. Any product is interchangeable if it follows the same semblance or usefulness with the product partner.

You and your partner can co-develop new products for both websites. To go back to the dog collar and dog tag business, if you both develop a collar that already has a tag on it without them being sold separately, then both of you could put the collar on the both sites and share the profit after manufacturing expenses have been factored out. Again, both parties win and both parties profit.

You can also invest in an Ezine partnership. This allows several partners to get together and promote each other's products on their websites. These partnerships should remain common. For example, if you are promoting an eBook on bipolar disorder, you could partner up with someone who has a product to help bipolar disorder or you could be advertised on other mental illness sites. In return you need to be able to advertise those other sites that promote yours. Make sure they are common thought. If your site promotes your book on bipolar disorder, you wouldn't want a lawn mower site advertising on your site and vise versa.

Commonality, reciprocation, and trust are the key components of a joint venture partnership. Go out and find all three attributes, and you will be able to increase your sales, increase your customer base, and increase your profits. The joint venture that you join into can make or break your business, so be careful and pick your partners carefully.

How Do You Know You Are Ready For An Online Joint Venture?

You are ready to join into a joint venture when you are ready to make money. You are ready when you have decided that you want to expand your customer base and expand your sales. You need a plan to maximize your initial investment and only get the customers that you know are interested in your product. Your future partner has to provide that site and also share in the same belief that a partnership will raise revenue for both parties. Without these want and attributes in place, then you need to rethink joint venture partnership.

You need to identify who your market is and what customers really want your product. Where are these customers? Are they set in one regional area or is your potential customer base on a world wide scale. You may have a good idea about your potential customers, but do they have the finances to pay for your product and come back for more when they need supplemental services?

You may have great demographics but without the revenue backing the want, you are out of business. For example, the demographics say that the country of Mexico is screaming for your product, but does that population have the financial means to purchase it. You would be wasting time and money trying to sell a product to a population that wants the product but can't afford it.

The next realization that you must come to is to figure out where you are right now in your sales and where you want to be. Is a joint venture wise at this time in your business plan or do you need to wait longer until the time is right? Look at where you and where you want to be in terms of profit, growth, and expansion. If you have a attainable goal, then you have to look at how you are going to get there. Is a joint venture the best opportunity you have right now at the lowest cost? Most of the times it is, but sometimes your business layout is not in the position to take up the responsibility of providing your partner with reciprocating services.

You need effective marketing knowledge to get to where you want to be and maybe, at this time, that knowledge is not there. This is when you need to seek that joint venture partner that has that knowledge and can share or use it for you. As part of the agreement, you can offer something to the partnership to compensate for your use of that knowledge. This can be in the form of more space on your site or a percentage of the sales that are generated from your partner's site. You have to give a little to equal up what you are lacking in the deal.

You have to have passion about your product to go into the joint venture world and your partner should have the same passion. You have to have a willingness to learn and even take a small loss to gain knowledge. If you partner up with someone that has extensive sales and marketing knowledge, keep your ears open and your mouth shut. Learn. The information shared either through communication or through the experience in the joint venturing partnership will help you through the next time you want to expand using the joint venture method. Don't be a know it all. Share what you know and help your partner and at the same time be willing to accept feedback and utilize it for your success.

Looking At The Joint Venture As A Process

When you are looking for a joint venture partner, you have to ask yourself, "What are they looking for?" You would think that they are looking for money from you to expand on their own needs and wants. This is not always true. Sometimes the joint venture partner wants a symbiotic relationship where both partners will benefit. They may need someone who is business savvy and can push their products in a new direction or expand their sales base. It is cheaper to have you as a partner, usually free, then hiring a marketing expert or even a secretary to hunt up leads and potential customers.

When you are dealing with a potential joint venture partner for the first time, don't jump right into bed with them, but feel them out for their potential sincerity. Never make a deal on a first meeting or on verbal interaction.

Get the information that you need verbally, and then ask them where to send the proposal for the joint venture. This will give them the idea that you are a legitimate business and that you are not going to be led by their ideas but your own. The written proposal will set down a legal back trail incase something goes negative in the relationship.

When you present your proposal in a written form, there are still some people in today's society that appreciates the written word instead of the electronic version. Their inboxes are probably filled everyday with other joint venture proposals and to receive a professional document by hand could be the edge to get the proposal looked at if not accepted. By slamming the internet full of proposals you are just another fish in the ocean trying to get fed. A well thought out and planned proposal will turn the eye of any serious future proposal.

You can find joint venture templates on the web using the template as a keyword. They are easy to download and fill out and they look professional. If you are really ambitious you might want to try to build your own form or use the templates as a guide to build your own unique form. Either way, you need to have your lawyer look at your proposal and make sure there are no loopholes that will come back to bite you in the future. A simple misspelling or a grammar error could cause you to lose a lot of money because of an ill worded proposal.

Once the proposal is submitted give it about three days after you think it would have been delivered. Call the prospective joint venture partner and ask if they have had a chance to go over it. If they have, be prepared to make amendments or other changes to make the partner happy. Have a copy of the proposal in front of you as you talk on the phone or run the document into a PDF file and you can conference call with Adobe to change the document online while both of you are looking at it. Before signing any changes, again have your lawyer look at it to make sure the changes did not destroy the integrity of the document.

Once Okayed and signed, be the first person to initiate the first phase of your project. Your partner may not have the time to jump right out there and initiate the start. By going the distance and starting the process yourself will instill more trust between partners.

Who To Go After As A Joint Venture Partner

Go for the big fish first. Don't waste your time going to a hundred companies that are the same size or smaller than you. If you land a big joint venture partner, it will overshadow the profit or the subscriber base you will find in a plethora of smaller ones. Don't be intimidated.

Most people are intimidated to submit a proposal to one on the internet giants. Because of this intimidation, many people do not try. By just sending a proposal to a big fish, you are stepping out from the crowd and you will be noticed for taking a chance.

Go after a joint venture product that has a like product as yours. You wouldn't want to sell fishing lures on a makeup site and vice versa. Look at the big fish, but the big fish that have a customer base that will match your market. If you take a fishing lure proposal to a make up company, you will be not only declined, but your integrity as a business man will be hurt. See what's out there. Make a list of all the companies out there that are similar to your product or service. Don't make it to big because you need to be able to keep control to who and where a proposal is going.

Once the list is made, put the companies in order from the biggest to the smallest. This can attained by the position they were in on the web page you pulled up with your product keyword. The first five positions mean that someone knows how to put their products out there with the right keywords and has enough internet savvy to market. Contact the people at the top of your list first. You might want to make a daily goal and send out five to ten proposals a day. Don't be discouraged if you get a negative reply or no reply at all. Keep plugging and soon you will find a joint venture partner worth waiting for.

Don't just rely on the internet to find possible joint venture partners. The most successful unions have been met in a bar or golf course. Get out and network. Tell people what you are doing and what you want to do.

It is amazing how many people you will find with a like mind that will be able to appreciate and help you find a partner or have the things and skills you need to become a partner themselves. Casual acquaintances that become business partners have had a track record of being more successful than just professional business junctures.

Once you put out your proposals, you might find that it is accepted by more than just one partner. Great! You do not have to be exclusive and it is sometimes unwise to sign an exclusive agreement with anyone. If you have five or six offers and they look like they will be beneficial to your company, then take them. The more joint ventures you have the more customer base you will have. You will have a chance to showcase a number of products on your sites that might lead to additional sales on yours. Think of ways you can incorporate your joint venture partners products with yours and with a little research and development, you and your partner could come up with a new product that both of you could feature and split the

Joint Ventures And Face To Face Encounters

You are on your way to work. You are sitting in a car and watching the pedestrians walk by. Unbeknownst to you, each person that is walking by could be a potential customer or joint venture partner. This amazing fact is true. The best way to find a joint venture partner is to get up close and personal. Face to face encounters is the best way to exchange ideas and to promote your product or service to be displayed on another person's website. A verbal exchange at a bar or in the locker room of your gym can give you the pre-knowledge of what the potential viability of that person being a joint venture partner.

There are several venues in which you can meet people of like mind and that are looking for a joint venture partner themselves. Trade shows and other gatherings are excellent places to find a joint venture partner, because that is what most trade shows and professional conferences are geared for. Have a pocket full of business cards on you and be prepared to talk and convince other people that your product or service is right for their needs. They then will try to convince you of the same thing. It is a booming opportunity in which you should include yourself every time you have a chance.

The trade shows are a benefit, but as a potential joint venture partner, you have to look at everyone you meet as a potential partner. If you are sitting at a restaurant alone at the bar, strike up a conversation with the person next to you. After pleasantries, ask the age old question, "So, what do you do?' You will be surprised at the number of people that you meet that are in the online marketing industry or at least has some kind of sideline that is in the market. It might not be but one or two out of ten people you meet, but that one or two could change your profit margin hugely.

When you press your product face to face, try not to sell the idea. Propose the idea and then ask how the other person thinks that the idea will be successful for them. Let their mind start to generate possibilities and dollar signs. It will be easier to go into a conversation with the potential partner if they are not of the defensive, but are thinking about how they are going to come out on top of the deal. Sit back and then when they start asking you questions, you can shine as you tell them how both of you can profit together.

Other social situations like parties get togethers, or family reunions can be an excellent source in finding potential joint venture partners. So what if you haven't seen Uncle Bob for ten years. Find out what he is doing now and how can his actions and business help promote yours. Get out, open your mouth and talk and ask questions. If you do not put your self out there and network.

It is reported that only 2% of all joint venture proposals sent by email are looked at. That is a very small percentage and you have to get out there and bring that percentage up. Email is fine, but the face to face encounter will build a joint venture partnership with personal interactions, trust, and eventually profit.

Three Key Elements to Making Your Online Joint Venture Successful

To be successful online, you and your joint venture partner needs to know what is steering the industry today. Most people call these secrets, but these secrets are out and you and your partner or potential partner needs to jump on the band wagon to be successful in the market. Most of these elements are free, but they do take a little time and effort to get them up and running. Using these three elements will have any joint venture partnership up and running to record sales and profits.

The first element that is essential is article marketing. This is a free add-on to your website that will draw millions of visitors to it. With this element, you need to write and submit articles to article submission sites that will draw the reader of the article to your product. By using keywords and listing your articles in various sites and using your website as a reference or a citation, you will be able to draw visitors to your site in droves. This will increase the number of inbound links to your page and then you will have a percentage of those readers actually become clients.

If you have little or no writing talent, there are many writing services out there that will write the articles for you for a fee. These articles can be stuffed with as many keywords as you wish and each keyword will not only bring the audience to the article, but link the article to your site.

Most writing services are reasonably priced and offer professional writing that will not only draw customers, but will give the readers worth while information that, again, will be passed on and draw more customers. It is a domino affect that will crash toward one goal, making your site more obtainable.

The second element to your joint venture project is to use Ezine publishing. This is like using the article based element but this requires you to provide your subscribers and your readers with valuable, enriching content that will give them a solution to their problems. The vitamin and supplement industry has used these Ezine articles successfully in the past because they give the cause, the treatment, and the cure of a certain person's personal problem. People are looking for answers and your Ezine publishing gives them those answers.

The third element to a successful joint venture is search engine optimization. This tool will drive not just traffic, but quality traffic to your website. You just have to know how to please the search engine gods. Again you have to use keywords throughout your content to 'optimize' your exposure. When the average Joe puts in the key word, bipolar disorder, the site that will come up first on the search pages is the site that uses the word bipolar more often throughout the page. Use the keywords in your article, title, and any tags that might people to your site.

These elements are good for a single website, but when used in a joint venture partnership, then the chances for customers and subscribers to come to either site is increased greatly. If you have multiple joint venture partners, these three elements used together can build a mighty business force that can hardly be reckoned with. Double the exposure means double the chances for increased sales and bigger profit.

Setting Up Competitive Barriers with Your Joint Venture Partner

Now that you have a joint venture partner, what can you and they do to capitalize on the partnership. Not only do you have to look at the customers and extra traffic you receive but you also have to look at what your competitors are doing and how you can beat them at the punch. You and your partner or partners can set up competitive barriers that will not allow competitors to catch up with your progress and at the same time you may flood the market with your product leaving them to catch the scraps. You will lead your and your partners to a level that is untouchable by people following in your footsteps.

The first step of setting up a competitive barrier is to find out exactly what your competitors are doing. If you are selling dog toys, then get on the internet and put in the keyword dog toys. Look at the first page of links that is presented. Look at how the page is set up. What key words are they using? What repetitive phrase or word do you see over and over? Look at how the page arranged. Is there keyword articles or links that will take you to an article or is there a search engine friendly phase that puts this at the top of the heap?

They are on the first page for a reason. They have already done what you are about to do so now you have to find a strategy to get your site on top. This may be adding more articles or keywords or finding a unique niche in which your site will be the prototype to follow. You may have to rework you marketing strategy, but with the help and the support of your joint venture partner you may have the volume to overcome the person you are trying to compete with. The more out of the box ideas you come up with, the more competitive you will be.

After finding out what the competition is doing right, find out what they are doing wrong. See if you can find a problem in their system like poor customer service or late deliveries. Whatever they are doing wrong you can do it right and maybe sway their traffic and customer base over to your site. If the competition is combining shipping costs for multiple orders, then you and your joint venture partner can devise a way to make shipping cheaper and more user friendly than your competitor. Since you have a larger customer base with your partner, you might be able to cut a deal with UPS or other package carriers that could undercut your competition.

The barriers of competition are a never ending cycle to remain top dog. As you are planning the demise of your competitor, you will have several people looking at your site and seeing if you are doing something right or wrong in which they can exploit. It sounds cut throat but it is apart of doing business. Sometimes your greatest competitor can become a joint venture partner themselves. This will eliminate the quest for their spot and you can focus on other people that are not apart of your joint venture network.

Competition breeds business. You must compete to survive in the business world whether your business is brick and mortar or virtual. The online environment is fierce and you have to be at the top of you game to survive. Surround yourself with good joint venture partners and the fight for customers will go easier with allies.

Tools For Picking Out The Right Joint Venture Partner For You

When trying to find a joint venture partner that is right for you, sometimes it takes weeks and maybe months of research to come up with the right partner, with the right customer base, with the right terms for your agreement. When you meet someone who might be a potential joint venture partner, you might get snowed if they are not on the up and up.

They can tell you that there site receives more traffic than it actually does or their keywords are not the ones that they claim. You find this out through time taking research, but there are tools out there where you can assess the website of your potential partner and assess the websites of your competitors.

www.copernic.com offers a great joint venture tool that not only contributes to the success of the joint venture partners, but also helps the solo entrepreneur find the partner in the first place. This device searches multiple search engines and uses keywords that you would find useful on your personal website. This takes all the guessing out of the keyword process and allows you to find the keywords that you need without taking a chance on using key words that don't. If the keywords that you choose match up with a potential partner, the tool will let you visit their website so you can contact them. All the pertinent information that you need to contact this person will be provided by the search tool.

Another great tool can be found at www.alexa.com. This fantastic tool downloads right on top of your browser and gives you the real time information that you need to know that you are picking the right joint venture partner. You will see how one site compares to another. So when you are making the list that will start you on the way of picking a joint venture partner, you will how one site ranks against another and you will be able to pick the ones that are the most desirable. The sites that have the greatest number of hits are yahoo.com and google.com. They would be listed in the top five. You would feel comfortable with picking a joint venture partner from those ranked one to one hundred thousand. Like the tool for www.copenic.com. You will also get the information that you need to contact the person to set up your joint venture deal.

Another wonderful asset to finding a joint venture partner is email. This is not a tool, but an essential in finding the right joint venture partner. The secret to email is to not to mass email or spam your potential partners, but to make each personal so that the potential partner will feel that you are taking a time to make a personal request for their time and potential partnership. Use group mail to personalize each of the mailings with the information that you have stored in your database. You will be able to store and use their personal contact information and the Ezine name. Just place in their name and personal information in the name tag and you will add that personal touch that will draw attention.

With these three tools and others that are out there, you can pinpoint that potential joint venture partner and know that they have the clout on the web to draw business to your site. You can also use the tools to keep a close eye on your competitors and find out what they are doing right and what they are doing wrong.

Creativity, Persistence, And Vision

To be successful in a joint venture partnership, you have to be motivated. There are three characteristics that you need to make it into the big leagues. Creativity, persistence, and vision are your keywords to success. You have to constantly think about these aspects to keep yourself on top of the game and on top of your competitor's moves. By combining these three elements you can be a leader in the field of your choosing and find and utilize the joint venture partner of your choosing.

Creativity is of the most important attributes you need to make your mark in the market and build the kind of business that will stand the test of time and competition. By thinking outside of the box and taking some risks on a new idea or concept, you are breaking the mold and moving into new territories that could be push you to the top. You have to see all angles of the business you are in and the angles that your joint venture partner has also. With all the angles considered, you can find a new niche in the market or find out that the joint venture partner that you have does not fit your purposes anymore and you need to find another partner that is more congruent.

You have to persistent in your efforts to align and realign yourself with productive joint venture partners. If one does not work out, you need to back out of the arrangement as politically as you can and find another partner that is more productive. Even if the lame duck partner is not producing much, keep them as a reserve because they may come up with an idea or concept that could skyrocket you into a higher realm. You have to stay on top of everything that is going on so that you can make the right decisions at the right time. You need to stay on top of proposals that you sent out so that your proposal does not get lost in the mix with the potential partner.

The vision that you possess is your greatest asset. Without vision, you have no goals or objectives to work toward. Your vision should be a shining trophy that you are constantly looking for and you must strive to reach the trophy every minute of your working day. The vision may become jagged or rearranged as you find new struggles in your quest, but the vision has to remain true in spite of bad deals, sour joint ventures, or a snag in your production and sales.

Keep your vision clear and true with making negotiations with a future joint venture partner. They may have good ideas, but if they take you away from your vision, then you will have to realign your vision or not take this partner seriously. Keep your customers in mind when making a deal. Is the overall process going to leave them with fewer services even though you are making the money? This may backfire in the end and your entire effort may crumble around you unless you keep your vision clear and your goals set. Changing goals in the middle of the game is fine, but do not let your future or current joint venture partner dictate the direction you are going. If you do change, make a sound redirection plan that will guarantee your success in the endeavor.

Joint Venture Partnerships Without You Having A Product

So you are internet savvy. You know how to market and to get a product out there, but you have no products to sell. That is okay. You can still form and develop a joint venture partnership that will be productive and make you money. It might be a little tougher than if you did have a product, but with perseverance and a little quick talking you can land that joint venture partnership that will be symbiotic and profitable. Therefore, you have to look at yourself differently. You are no longer selling a product, you are selling the service and that joint venture partner now has a chance to use your skills, instead of some product that you are selling.

First you have to find a business partner with a product that matches your skills. If you do not know anything about financing, you probably do not want to align yourself with a joint venture partner that deals with stocks or bonds. You probably want to go with a partner that has a product that you are familiar with and that you know that you can market correctly. Look at other people's websites. Look at what you could do to improve them. Contact the webmaster with your ideas and make a proposal that is both doable and is profitable for both parties involved.

Now that you have determined what you can offer a potential joint venture partner, you have to decide what you want from them. Think about a fair deal. Don't try to gouge your potential partner. They probably know what you are worth and if you try to get over on them it could harm your deal making prowess. Write a formal business plan that will address all issues, negative and positive, and that will address all foreseeable problems that might arise. You may also think about putting in an exit strategy if you or your partner feels that the deal in not working and one or both of you want out.

Another way to enter a joint venture without products is to find someone with products to sell but no venue. This could be done locally or at a trade show where you find local businesses that have the stock that they need moved and do not have the internet experience to move it. Here again you sell yourself as the product. You do not have to have a storehouse of merchandise or a catalog of electronic texts to push. All you need to be successful is the means to open a highway of commerce for that business man who does not know how to do it for themselves.

When you have no product, the product is you. If you do not know what you are good at or what you have a niche for that sells, sit down and write out a comprehensive list that lists all your good attributes that might be worth selling. Start writing them down in a professional manner so that you can show the future joint venture partner that you are experienced and you have the skills to move their product. Just like a writer aspiring to get a new job. They have to show a copy of their work to their potential employer to prove they have skills and knowledge to be a valuable asset to the company. Your skills are your resume and are sellable, just like any other product on the market.

Using Free Products To Use As A Joint Venture

How do you obtain free products to sell on your website for a profit? Join venture marketing has created a venue to obtain free electronic products such as eBooks and Ezines that are given by the authors for free, in exchange for their appearance on your website. Labeled as Master Resell Right's products and Private Label Rights products, these items can increase traffic to your website and at the same time provide a venue for the marketer? These products are ready to go and need no shipping and handling. You simply accept payment and download the material to your client.

The benefit to both joint venture partners is evident. You receive products to put on your website and they provide the products. When a product sells, according to the agreement made, you will receive a portion of the profits as a advertising agent and the author of the e-material will receive a portion for the creative rights of his or her product. You are essentially a bill board in cyberspace. Where a billboard provides a rental fee, you provide the avenue to push the product and to get the product noticed by your subscriber base.

The negative thing about this kind of joint venture is that you are using your client base and your partner does not have one from which you can draw. It is one sided when you are looking at the partnership from the traditional joint venture view. You would normally get your product exposed to their customer base, but in this endeavor you stand alone on product distribution. You are only the carrier of the product, and your products will remain on your site without any extra exposure.

The positive thing about this one sided joint venture is that you could make a lot of money of the commission of the sold e-texts on your site. If your author is savvy to keywords and has an article that is of great public interest, then not only will those keywords drive the market to your site, but you are reciprocated when they by the e-text. For example if an author wrote an e-text like a common subject about how to lose weight or how to improve a relationship, then you would get the common responses to those looking to fix their plight. If the author has found a special niche in the market that will drive people to purchasing the information offered, then your market base will spread and you website will receive higher number of hits.

In the agreement, you might have to pay the provider of the e-texts with a portion of the profits that you have made because of their product on your website. Then can be hard to prove sometimes, but if you have an accurate representation of what you were pulling in before the product was listed on your site and what you are pulling in afterwards, then you would have a guideline to barter for an interest agreement. You can even add customers by having them sign up for your websites newsletter before they receive the product that your partner is selling them. This will replace the data that you are missing from the traditional joint venture. These types of partnerships are risky if you do not know what you are doing during the proposal stage. Ask advice from professionals and have your lawyer look at the contract beforehand.

More Benefits of Joint Marketing Ventures

As you have learned in this text there are many benefits to joint venture partners and marketing. This next chapter will detail and expand on those benefits so you as the reader can pick out the good points that you want to stress during your joint venture partner proposal and implementation of your project. You can be a devil's advocate on any of these points, but if you have the three pre-mentioned attributes, creativity, persistence, and vision, you will see that each benefit will work for you in any circumstance.

In a joint marketing venture, you can build long lasting relationships that will be beneficial for both partners for a long time to come. As the market changes and fluxuates and new marketing ideas and implications are presented, you can ebb and flow as a tide to meet the new challenges and become unified as a team that will succumb. A longer relationship has stronger trust bonds and they intricacies of your partnership will make your venture be able to problem solve faster and be able to meet the demands placed on your market and your products.

You can increase you credibility by teaming up with someone that already has a creditable reputation in the business. If your partner has a good reputation and a solid customer base, then you will be guilty of having the same through association with this partner. His credit and his track record will become yours as you stand the test of time and become associated with his site. You will reap the benefits from every good thing that is accomplished or every customer that is satisfied. In return, that partner will also reap the same thins from you as your credibility grows.

As mentioned previously, you can receive free products such as e-commerce and more tangible items to present and to sell on your site. This relationship takes a little more planning, but he extra traffic sent to your site will allow you to pick up the lost space on your page with profit. If you are doing the 'billboard' type partnership, then you will be free of storage and other things that have to do with a tangible product. You don't have to worry about shipping and handling. All you have to do is wait for the revenue to start pouring into your bank account.

The real benefit is that you can construct most proposals and joint venture deals with little or no money. You are trading e-space and a customer base, not anything that can be handed to each other except for the monetary residuals that are the most important thing. Joint venture deals can be created so that you just have to expend the time to create them. Once posted and presented on the website, the only work you have to do is fill the orders or exchange the residuals between the partners.

The main reason for a joint venture deal is the main benefit. That is to gain new leads and customers. A joint venture deal may be one-sided and you may have the bigger customer base, but if you look at things in the long run, you probably are the small fish to a bigger partner on another deal. You win through statistics on the long haul. Just watch yourself and don't put to many one-sided deals against you. Even out the playing field and balance yourself with both sides of the equation to give you a solid foundation if a partner was to back out of the deal.

With a solid joint venture partnership you can gain get discounts on products or services. Previously mentioned, if you have a service you can provide to a partner, you don't have to have any products to sell or trade, just you and your toolbox. The same goes the other way. You might receive a free service that will help boost your traffic and your sales and you do not have to put their product on your site. You use them and they will promote their service. Your product will be on their site and their service will be on yours.

With joint venture partnerships you can save a lot of money on your business and your business operating costs. For example, if you were only selling your products on the your site, you would have to pay for the entire operating costs of promoting that website and delivering bought items. With the revenue earned through your venture partner, you will have your website operating expenses paid for or at least reduced by the income generated from your partner's endeavors. Plus the extra income generated from your products on their site will also break down you operating costs. Beating the competition is the best feeling and a valuable benefit of joint venture partnerships.

If you can weed out the competition, or at least slow them down, your website and that of your partners will reap the benefits of added traffic and revenue. Your partnership will be much stronger and have added resources to compete effectively in the open market. What resources you don't have, your partner may and this may be enough to effectively withstand any competitor's tactics to bring you down. There is strength in numbers and as in battle, so it is in business.

A real advantage of a joint venture partnership is that you can gain referral for other businesses. If your partner is linked to several other partners that you don't even know about, the increase in your partner's site in reference to customers will increase. Because of the other partners, which you are not apart of, his site will reach new traffic records. But because you are apart of his website his gains are your gains. If he has a thousand new hits, you can guarantee that you will be able to pull a significant gain from their fortune.

The time you save with a joint venture is almost enough to cut money out of the equation itself. With time you can enjoy the quality of life that you expect as a self-imposed businessman. You can spend time with family and friends, while the partnerships that you make take some of the load off your shoulders.

Your business problems will be solved faster with the help from your partner and they will also benefit from your website. It is a win-win situation all the way around and the both the partners benefit from the relationship. More time and less money equal profitability in both the realms of the health of your bank account and the health of your body and mind. It just makes sense to share the burdens of business but also to share the benefits of business. With joint venture marketing and the right joint venture partners. Your business and your health will be better in the long run.

When To Enter A Joint Venture With Caution

As mentioned previously in this text, you really have to research your potential partner when considering a joint venture. Ask for references and see some samples of their work and profitability before you take the plunge and share your business bed with an unknown person. Get proof of their past successes and make sure that the proof is not bogus or made up. Also make sure that what they are offering you is real. You might want to go undercover and buy from their site to see what kind of service or product you get from them.

The opposite is true. Sometimes it is bad to know you perspective partner too well. Stay away from family members because of this. A bad partnership will spill over to a bad family relationship. Just because Uncle Bob has a good idea, a good website, and good traffic doesn't mean that either you or him will at sometimes come to a disagreement about business that could spill over to your family relationship. You may lose your business, but your family relationships last, or should last forever. If you use a family member be very careful and have the proposal and agreement zoned with a really good exit strategy that will end the deal before it ends the personal relationship.

Your really close friends are subject to turn on you if they are involved in a joint venture with you. No matter how thick the blood or ties you have with a friend, they are easily swayed to go their own direction when the business deal sours. Then you loose out on both the friendship and the business possibilities that you both share. Make sure that you are willing to risk both when looking at a close friend for a business excursion. They may be like a brother, but money and time investment can ruin a friendship for life if it sours.

It is just human nature to trust family and friends. You might inadvertently forget a step in the proposal process that will come back in bite you in the butt in the future. You might overlook their lack of skill in the business or their devotion to the partnership because you have an unyielding trust toward the individual.

The balance is an easy one to maintain. You can find a partner that you know well enough to trust with a business relationship, but the key is to not know them well enough that a personal relationship will be damaged. The same goes true for existing partners. If you and your partner develop a relationship that goes beyond the agreement that you initially start with, then you have a potential volatile situation in which that relationship, both business and personal, will be damaged. You have to find a compatible partner in which you are willing to let go if the need arises.

You both have a common vision and a common goal to work together. Your Uncle Bob may want the same things that you want, but is he really going to work hard to get there. The added question do you have enough gumption to confront your Uncle or are you going to continue the business relationship though you are losing money and time. It's a tough decision and this is something you have to think about before you

How To Avoid Legal Issues In Your Joint Venture

In a joint venture proposal, you have to plan, plan, and plan some more. You need three important components of the proposal and the actual agreement and the most important thing about all three is to have the documents in written word and not a verbal agreement. If you follow these rules, your legal hassles will not come to fruitation or will be very minimal. You have to make sure that both parties sign the agreement and acknowledge it as a legal document and not just a locker room partnership. This will protect you and you will profit more with this assurance in writing.

The first thing you need to have is a joint venture agreement. This will provide a contract between you and your partner that is binding and legal. The document will spell out the reason and the purpose of the joint venture and the responsibilities of each partner during the duration of the agreement. The time allotted for the venture is also included in the agreement and a time allotted for an exit strategy incase one partner wants out is also outlined. The most important aspect of the joint venture agreement is that you decide how the revenue and profit is decided.

Make sure that you have a legal representative from both parties look at the agreement. The document should be revised and reconstructed until both parties and their legal representatives are happy. Don't use the same lawyer. Each partner should have their own legal representative to look at their interests specifically. If you share legal counsel, the counsel might side with one or the other of you and you might end up on the losing end of the deal.

If you draft the agreement with the partner, have a checklist ready so that each of you can check off as a potential problem or benefit of the partnership. To get your future partner's perspective could open up your creative spirits and let you see new aspects of the partnerships and new benefits that might come your way.

Also if you build the agreement jointly, all of your interests will be covered and the amount of revenue that you receive will be set in stone.

The second part of the process to keep you out of trouble legally is a business plan. Not just as a business plan, but a sound business plan. This document will spell out the goals and the objectives of your joint venture and the path you need to take to get there. In this document you will discuss if funding is need for the project and if the project needs funds at all. If there are loans, investments, or other financial considerations, this is the time that you would jot down your concerns and your expectations.

Even if you do not have to fund anything and the agreement is free for both parties, you still need a good plan to carry out and meet your business goals. This document is the one that both you and your partner will look at to either rekindle a new interest or to makes sure the other side of the table is holding up their side of the agreement. This is also the agreement that you will use if you have to seek the financial help of a lending institution or bank. They will use the business plan as a decision maker to see whether you are sound enough to lend money to or not.

Most business plans are complex and if you are not a competent writer you may word something in a way that you may not wish to. This will leave you open to speculation and you may leave a loophole in which you or your lawyer cannot fill. You may leave yourself out to hang unless you hire a professional writer that is used to writing business proposals. Professional writers are abundant on the web and the keywords freelance or free lance writing will land you the person that can write you document in a professional and legal manner.

If your business plan is strong and your proposal is right, you will probably not have a problem with your partnership. If things go wrong, you need a strong exit strategy that will get both parties out of the partnership with little to no trouble. You or your partner may find a new marketing approach that will invalidate your agreement. If suddenly you receive ten thousand or more hits on your site and are receiving very little from his. The partnership is not out of balance and your partner is getting more profit from your efforts. It is time to realign the relationship or you need to get out of the deal.

If you have to get out, you have to have a viable, realistic exit strategy. You need to know when to get out and how to get out of the partnership. It should both be written in your proposal and in your business plan. Your partner should not be surprised about you using an exit strategy and you should not be surprised when they use it either. The guidelines and goals should be set so both parties know when one of the either of you get in a position where the table have turned it is not profitable to be in the partnership anymore.

You are setting yourself up for failure if you go into a joint venture on a verbal agreement. Verbal agreements are very hard to prosecute and defend in a court of law. You and your partner will both lose time and money if you end up in a legal dispute. Joint venturing is a new concept when you throw in the internet and a lot of the laws and legal consoling have not caught up to the new idea. That is why you need an air tight proposal, business plan, and exit strategy. If one link of these three in the chain is weak, your entire joint venture partnership will be weak.

Remember to plan your strategy. Write it down in the proposal and to make sure that legal consul has read and improved it. Your business plan needs to be well rounded and secure. You can add or detract goals as necessary as your partnership matures and your objectives or dynamics of your business changes. This is the natural evolution of business, so don't let it shock you system. Just go with the flow and you will find yourself a person that has a successful business due to your professional endeavors with a joint venture partnership.

Personal Success Stories With Joint Venture Partners

That's One Spicy Sauce!

Starting out with just a blog and a passion for hot sauce, Nick Lindauer is a true example of an online success story. Lindauer started his now profitable business by hand out of his apartment while in college. Just starting the online store Sweat 'N' Spice he did everything by hand. He would make, package, and ship the orders himself. Not exactly a high rolling business to start with, in fact Sweat 'N' Spice hardly made a profit in the starting year of 2001. Since then, through online advertising, word of mouth, and a popular blog site called hotsauceblog.com in which Lindauer manages, the company has made quite a surge. Lindauer now pushes over a thousand products from various companies.

With their rise in popularity, Lindauer has branched out from just selling hot sauce, though still his number one passion. Sweat 'N' Spice also markets spices, relishes, and snacks. How does this company compete with other manufacturers? Sweat 'N' Spice present their products in a unique as well as tasty fashion. The company puts flair in their product containers by making bottles in fun and funky shapes, attributes interesting names to their products, and even acquires celebrities to endorse products.

Lindauer offers a variety of pricing options that range from reasonable to high depending on what the customer is looking for. You can get some hot sauce for your next get together, or buy a limited edition sauce for a hefty price, kind of resembles that of the wine market. By building his business to offer such a variety and through well a well designed blog site, Lindauer has built a profit that exceeds $130,000 yearly. Quite an amazing realization that began with a simple college experiment, and expanded into a very profitable and ever growing business.

Fashion Is A Must

How on earth does a person get an online business started? Obviously having a great product wasn't helpful if it couldn't be marketed. Amber realized that trying to just sell her personally designed purses on word-of-mouth alone was not working. This was evident by the stockpile of inventory sitting in the house that also acted as a temporary storage for her designs. The inventory wasn't moving except for a small number here and there. That's when Amber Stockton partnered with longtime friend and current business partner Rachel. Amber describes Rachel as an unofficial internet genius.

Rachel was a stay at home mom who had the time and knowledge to commit to Amber's new business venture. Rachel recognized the potential in a purse that offered the sense of simplicity with the combination of great fashion. Especially for busy moms, having a purse that offers a variety of compartments with the hand's free luxury is a must. Having the option of all that in addition to a compact but fashionable design is hard to find, especially on a lesser budget. Splitting the cost of an internet domain site, Rachel did all the leg work in developing an operative web site that would launch the new business. Amber supplied the goods and Rachel supplied the know-how. With the help of online marketing, local advertising, and word of mouth, there was a rapid increase in business. Being fortunate enough to have our local new channel promote a story, sales began to soar.

Amber and Rachel not only made a profit in the first year, they proved that with a marketable idea and great partnership, anything is possible. After two years of business their clientele has increased with the sky rocket of highly pleased customers. They now distribute their product all over the United States. Who knows, that fashionable purse that you admired just might be the product designed and produced by Amber and Rachel.

You Sell Butterflies?

When people think of products that can be sold rarely do they think of insects. Normally thoughts turn to food, clothing, and other goods. Fortunately for one man and a bet between friends, he profited off the idea of selling butterflies online. Yes, butterflies, and believe it or not it's quite a profitable business.

Jose Muñiz began the thriving business of selling butterflies n 1999 with the help of his business partner and wife, Karen.

Starting out small the two began advertising their services to weddings, charities, business events, and funerals. Since the humble beginnings the company properly named Amazing Butterflies has grown dramatically to meet the needs of their thriving business. There are Florida, California, and now Texas. Amazing Butterflies have been featured in many publications such as Brides, Modern Bride, Martha Stewart Weddings, Premier Bride, Ritz Carlton Weddings, Orange County Bride, Bridal Guide, as well as many more.

Jose Muniz has clearly been successful in winning his bet as well as turning the $100 bet in to a million dollar company. Amazing Butterflies not only provides the service of shipping butterflies, they also offer plants in which the butterflies can thrive on, artwork, apparel, and furniture. Not only has Jose Muniz and Karen made a profit on their business venture, they have found something that they love to do. Just goes to show that not every business venture has to be manufactured per say. Sometimes it just take a great idea, great partnership, and using what's already been provided by nature.

Music Enthusiast Make Big

Who knew that having a love of music and the knowledge of iPods would come in handy? Evidently Barry recognized the opportunity with this type of technology know how. He gets paid for transferring songs to customer's IPods. Barry came up with the idea when he transferred songs for himself as well as family members and friends. Barry realized that there was a need for such services to the many that lack the knowledge or don't have the time for a task such as this.

Although to not an expert in the field of music Barry still has a lot to learn. With music taste that varies hugely, Barry is devoted to doing the research it takes to satisfy customers. Teaming with business partner and Sister Sandra who is also a music enthusiast, the duo has been quite successful in advertising their services to a vast population. In turn the customers have been pouring in. The business partners have had to work full time in order to keep up with demand.

By charging reasonable prices for the provided services, Barry and Sandra have many returning customers that were pleased with services in the past. Although still being a new, it has already been recognized that they have stumbled into a lucrative business. For the first year in business they are projecting profits up to $100,000 and up to $150,000 for the next. The company is looking for possible expansion into commercial office space eventually, but for now is content with the profitable home business. Sometimes business with family is a winning combination.

Home With the Kids and Still Working

Just because a person chooses to stay home with their kids doesn't mean that they no longer have a money making career. Although raising kids is definitely a full time job, there are ways to make a profit while staying at home. So how does the average stay at home mom or dad make a little bit of extra income? Really, it depends on an individual's talents as well as motivation, but one mom found the secret.

Raising kids full time had Michelle surfing the internet daily in order to find answers to questions varying in range and topic. On day while spending time on the computer Michelle figured that there must be a way to profit while surfing in cyber space. She spoke to neighbor and long time friend Marianne who agreed and they both set out to come up with a solution. Both mothers agreed that they wasted a lot of time trying to find answers pertaining to their kids due to having to do various searches for the different answers. In that single moment of agreement came the idea a of their new business venture.

Since they had both done the motherhood thing more than once, they decided they would provide a website that would compile all their well researched information into one source. Doing the research that was required and compiling into one source they in turn created a parent friendly site that answered all imaginable questions pertaining to children and the raising of them. Marianne and Michelle also added little tidbits learned firsthand through the years as well.

With the website complete they then aggressively advertised to companies who for a small fee could advertise on their site. After all, why not turn their unpaid at home job of being a full time mother into a profit. In very little time they had a highly popular site that was also helpful and informative for parents in all aspects of life. The two used firsthand knowledge and real life experience to become successful in their online joint venture. As with many, not only do they profit from their business, they fully enjoy it.

What Have We Learned About Joint Venture Partnerships

You have read almost twenty plus pages about joint venture partnerships and the benefits that they can bring your business. Whether you have been online for several years or have just plugged in today, you have the potential of making huge amounts of money in a very short period of time. You can partner yourself up with larger companies and each partner will act as a beneficiary of the other. You will succeed with the proper precautions and planning with little or no money out of your pocket. Your website will develop more traffic and your sales will increase.

Now that you understand joint venture partnerships and are excited about getting out there and forming new business relationships, you need to take a close look at your business and your business goals. Don't just sit and think for an hour or two. Spend days going over where you are now, where you want to be, and how you are going to get there. Write it all down and look at several goals or objectives to get you where you need to be. Put the goals in a sequential order that will make sense to you and sense to your potential partner.

Use your goals to emphasize your products and services. This should give you an idea of where you need to go to find a joint venture partner that is compatible with your business. Start your research of partners. Use the tools that will really give you their place and traffic in the internet world and find a partner that has a high traffic record, good credibility, and a customer base that will benefit you. Make sure that you spend a lot of time on the research phase. A bad partner could make or break your business if you are not careful or you do not do your research carefully.

Once you have your potential partners lined up, send them a 'personal' proposal that will get their attention and relay upon them that you are the genuine article. Make your proposal legal and make sure it is written down. No verbal agreements. Make sure that you and your partner know exactly what you are agreeing on before you sign a business plan or other binding agreement. Use your legal consul, not theirs but yours. Don't share legal consul at all.

The way you approach your joint venture adventure is your choosing. Hopefully this document has shown you the pitfalls and benefits of joint venture marketing and joint venture partnerships. As with any business dealing, just plan ahead and use your head. The profit is out there. Willing partners are out there. You just have to make a plan, do the research, stick to the plan and meet your business aspirations.

All will fall into place when you execute your plan with a degree of professionalism. Listen to your potential partners and learn from them. Knowledge and use of that knowledge sells your products and builds your traffic and customer base. Everyone you meet is a potential customer, but is also a potential partner that has the resources you need and perhaps the knowledge to put you over the top in your financial and your business goals.

www.ingramcontent.com/pod-product-compliance
Lightning Source LLC
LaVergne TN
LVHW021054100526
838202LV00083B/5911